LATVIA

LATVIA

THEN & NOW

Prepared by
Geography Department

Lerner Publications Company
Minneapolis

Series editors: Mary M. Rodgers, Tom Streissguth,
  Colleen Sexton
Photo researcher: Bill Kauffmann
Designer: Zachary Marell

Our thanks to the following people for their help in
preparing and checking the text of this book: Dr. Craig
ZumBrunnen, Department of Geography, University of
Washington; Keith Eliot Greenberg; and the American
Latvian Association of the United States.

Pronunciation Guide

baigais gad	BAY-gayz GADS
dianas	DIE-ee-nahs
glasnost	GLAZ-nost
Kurzeme	KOOR-zeh-may
Kyrghyzstan	keer-GEEZ-stan
Lacplesis	LATCH-plee-sihs
Lielupe	LEE-el-uh-pay
Liepāja	LEE-eh-pay-yah
trejdeksnis	TREEYEH-decks-nihs
Ziemas Svetki	ZEE-eh-mas SVET-key

Words in **bold** type are listed in a glossary that starts on page 52.

LIBRARY OF CONGRESS CATALOGING-IN-PUBLICATION DATA

Latvia / prepared by Geography Department, Lerner Publications Company.
     p. cm. — (Then & now)
   Includes index.
   Summary: Discusses the geography, history, ethnography,
resources, politics, and future of this Baltic country, annexed
by the Soviet Union in 1940 and independent once again in
1991.
   ISBN 0-8225-2802-9 (lib. bdg.)
   1. Latvia—History—Juvenile literature. [1. Latvia.] I. Lerner
Publications Company. Geography Dept. II. Series: Then &
now (Minneapolis, Minn.)
DK504.56.L38 1992
947'.43—dc20   92-7260
                                                    CIP
                                                    AC

Manufactured in the United States of America
1 2 3 4 5 6 7 8 9 10 01 00 99 98 97 96 95 94 93 92

• CONTENTS •

INTRODUCTION • 7

CHAPTER ONE
The Land and People of Latvia • 11

CHAPTER TWO
Latvia's Story • 27

CHAPTER THREE
Making a Living in Latvia • 39

CHAPTER FOUR
What's Next for Latvia? • 47

GLOSSARY • 52

INDEX • 55

At a park in Riga, the capital of Latvia, a young girl wears warm clothing to protect herself against cold temperatures.

"There has been a total turnaround in people's thinking . . . . It amounts to a historic national awakening."

Dainis Ivans
President of the Popular Front
April 1989

In 1992, the Soviet Union would have celebrated the 75th anniversary of the revolution of 1917. During that revolt, political activists called **Communists** overthrew the czar (ruler) and the government of the **Russian Empire.** The revolution of 1917 was the first step in establishing the 15-member **Union of Soviet Socialist Republics (USSR).**

The Soviet Union stretched from eastern Europe across northern Asia and contained nearly 300 million people. Within this vast nation, the Communist government guaranteed housing, education, health care, and lifetime employment. Communist leaders told farmers and factory workers that Soviet citizens owned all property in common. The new nation quickly **industrialized,** meaning it built many new factories and upgraded existing ones. It also modernized and enlarged its farms. In addition, the USSR created a huge, well-equipped military force that made it one of the most powerful nations in the world.

Latvians leave flowers beneath Riga's Freedom Monument in honor of those who died in the struggle against Soviet rule. The structure was built in 1935, during Latvia's first period of independence.

By the early 1990s, the Soviet Union was in a period of rapid change and turmoil. The central government had mismanaged the economy, which was failing to provide goods. To control the various ethnic groups within the USSR, the Communists had long restricted many freedoms. People throughout the vast nation were dissatisfied.

Several republics were seeking independence from Soviet rule—a development that worried some old-style Communist leaders. In August 1991, these conservative Communists used Soviet military power to try to overthrow the nation's president. Their effort failed and hastened the breakup of the USSR.

Latvia, a small, low-lying nation in north central Europe, had won its freedom from the Russian Em-

On top of the Freedom Monument, a figure representing liberty holds up a ring made of three five-pointed stars. They stand for three historic regions of Latvia—Kurland, Livonia, and Latgale.

A vendor in Riga offers radishes and other vegetables for sale.

pire after the 1917 revolution. But Latvian independence lasted only until 1940, when Soviet forces invaded and **annexed** the country. For 50 years thereafter, Latvia remained an occupied part of the USSR.

In the late 1980s, huge crowds of Latvian demonstrators demanded democracy and an end to Soviet rule. New leaders and a new parliament came to power in 1990, when Latvia again declared its independence. Soviet forces stationed in the country attacked Latvian protesters and occupied an important government office. After the failed attempt to overthrow the Soviet president, however, the Republic of Latvia gained recognition from many foreign states. In the fall of 1991, Latvia joined the **United Nations** as a free and self-governing country.

Latvian students take the long way home to enjoy ice-cream cones.

CHAPTER ONE

The Land and People of Latvia

F or centuries, Latvian children have delighted in *Lacplesis*, the story of a powerful boy whose mother was a bear. In the late 1980s, Latvian adults also became fascinated by *Lacplesis*, and the country's musicians created a rock opera based on the fable. Audiences thrilled to the opera's dramatic ending, when the boy kills a bear that threatens his father.

No longer just a children's tale, *Lacplesis* had become a reflection of current events. The bear was now the "Russian bear" and represented the government of the Soviet Union, which had ruled Latvia since 1940. The brave boy who risked his life for his family became a symbol of the new generation of Latvians seeking freedom from Soviet rule.

In a nation that had long been occupied by outsiders, *Lacplesis* inspired the belief that the bad years would soon end. In 1991, when countries around the world recognized Latvia as an independent state, many Latvians believed their hopes had

The buildings on Riga's Meistaru Street display some of the capital's historic architectural styles.

One of Latvia's worst environmental problems is the pollution of the Baltic Sea. Here, a Latvian activist has placed flowers in the sea as a memorial to clean water. The blossoms are the same colors as the Latvian national flag.

come true. Economic, environmental, and political problems are still widespread in Latvia. From now on, however, Latvians—not outsiders—will determine the fate of their country.

• Topography and Climate •

Latvia lies on the eastern shore of the Baltic Sea, an arm of the North Atlantic Ocean. The Gulf of Riga forms a wide, curving inlet along Latvia's northwestern seacoast. To the north of Latvia is Estonia, and to the south is Lithuania. Because these three countries border the Baltic Sea, they are known as the **Baltic States.** The Scandinavian nations of Sweden and Finland lie to the west and north, respectively, across the Baltic Sea.

Directly east of Latvia is Russia, a former enemy and now a strong supporter of Latvian independence. Bordering Latvia to the south is Belarus,

Ballet dancers perform at a theater in Riga.

which was also a Soviet republic before the summer of 1991. Latvia covers 25,400 square miles (65,786 square kilometers) of territory, an area equal to the size of West Virginia or of Belgium and the Netherlands combined.

A relatively low and flat country, Latvia makes up part of the large East European Plain that stretches along the coast of the Baltic Sea. The highest point in Latvia is a hill that reaches 1,024 feet (312 meters) above sea level. Four major rivers—the Daugava, Venta, Gauja, and Lielupe—run through the country.

Silver birch, aspen, maple, and oak trees flourish along Latvia's 308-mile (496-km) Baltic coast. Forests and isolated groves cover nearly one-half of the land, but there is also a great deal of open, fertile farmland. About 4,000 lakes dot the countryside. Many of the marshes and bogs that existed in ancient times remain in both coastal and interior regions.

Young Latvians play in a vegetable patch that is part of their family's farm. Animals and crops thrive in the country's level, fertile fields.

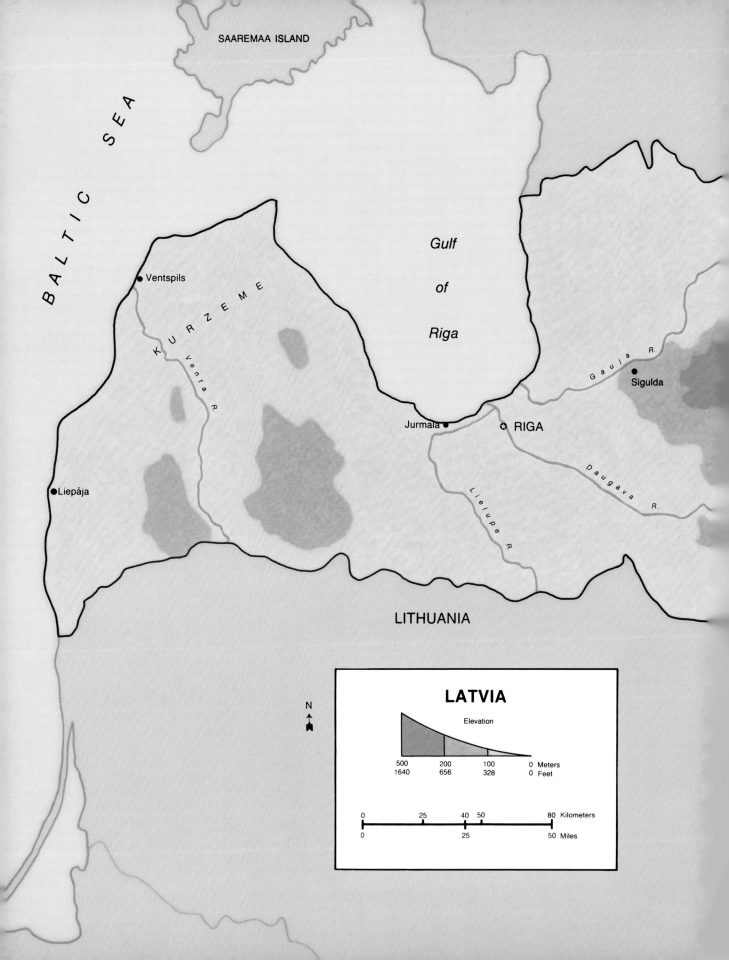

SAAREMAA ISLAND

BALTIC SEA

Gulf
of
Riga

● Ventspils

K U R Z E M E

Venta R.

● Liepāja

Gauja R.

● Sigulda

Jurmala ● ✪ RIGA

Lielupe R.

Daugava R.

LITHUANIA

N

LATVIA

Elevation

500	200	100	0 Meters
1640	656	328	0 Feet

| 0 | 25 | 40 50 | 80 Kilometers |

| 0 | 25 | 50 Miles |

ESTONIA

RUSSIA

◇ Gaizina Kalns

● Daugavpils

BELARUS

A *grove of birch trees lines a highway that carries traffic to Riga. Woodlands blanket nearly half of Latvia.*

FORMER USSR

LATVIA

Although Latvia is as far north as Juneau, Alaska, the warm currents from the North Atlantic Ocean bring the country mild temperatures. Riga, the capital city, has an average summer temperature of 64° F (18° C). In the winter, the Gulf of Riga freezes over, while the warmer waters of the Baltic Sea enable ports to stay open in the Kurzeme region of western Latvia. Riga's average temperature in January, the coldest month, is 20° F (–6° C). The country's annual rainfall is about 22 inches (56 centimeters).

Founded in the early 13th century, Riga is laced with twisting cobblestone streets and dotted with red-tiled roofs. Although the Soviet occupation left much of the city in disrepair, work is under way to restore historic parts of the capital to their former state.

Autumn leaves are caught in the crossed sticks of a Latvian fence.

Young Latvians line up for a school outing in Riga.

• Cities •

Most important events in Latvia take place in Riga, a city of one million residents—or one-third of the country's total population. In 1201, German **crusaders** (religious soldiers) founded Riga, which developed into a wealthy city of merchants and traders. In the early 20th century, Riga became an important industrial hub of the Baltic region.

Much of the older city center has survived intact despite centuries of invasion and occupation. Civic and religious buildings in Riga date as far back as the 14th century, and the spires of six old churches still rise above the city's skyline.

Although Riga is the nation's capital, **ethnic Latvians** make up only a third of the city's population. Riga's Russian-speaking residents—who held the most important jobs during the Soviet occupation—are still in the majority. Many of these Russians do not speak Latvian, but most want to remain residents of an independent Latvia.

LATVIA'S FIGHT FOR CLEAN AIR

Latvia is one of the most industrialized republics in the former USSR. After World War II (1939–1945), when the Soviet occupation was in force, Latvia experienced the rapid development of all types of manufacturing facilities. These new factories routinely poured harmful chemical pollutants—including sulfur dioxide, nitrogen oxide, and ammonia—into the air through smokestacks. The firms that operated these factories did not modernize their equipment or install effective pollution controls. As a result, Latvia's air quality is now among the worst in all the former Soviet republics.

Latvia's air pollution may be causing health problems for some of the nation's citizens. In urban areas, for example, the rates of cancer, breathing ailments, and skin diseases are high. Ventspils—a port on the Baltic Sea that has chemical plants and a gasoline refinery—suffers from severe air pollution. Many women in Ventspils travel elsewhere to have their babies to minimize the risk of birth defects. Local authorities distribute gas masks to children to protect them from the poisoned air, and tourists are advised to avoid the city if possible.

Air pollution can also harm plants and animals that live far away from urban areas. Pollutants combine with rain to make an acidic solution—called **acid rain**—that falls on rural forests, lakes, and rivers. Some lakes polluted with acid rain have stopped supporting life of any kind.

In the late 1980s, newly formed environmental groups began to educate Latvians about the causes and hazards of industrial pollution. Freed of central Soviet control, the independent Latvian government can now work directly with industry and environmentalists to clean up the nation's air.

Latvia's second largest city is Daugavpils (population 127,000). It sits on the banks of the Daugava River in eastern Latvia at a strategic crossroads in the Baltic region. Railroads link the city with Poland, Lithuania, Belarus, and Russia. Regional trade caused the rapid growth of Daugavpils in the 20th century, but the arrival of Russian industrial workers overwhelmed the city's Latvian population. Ethnic Latvians now make up only 10 percent of the population of Daugavpils.

The largest city in western Latvia, Liepāja (population 114,000) lies on the shores of the Baltic Sea. The city once boasted close communications and transportation links with western Europe and is still the site of an important former Soviet naval base. Also a busy cultural hub, Liepāja hosts a popular rock festival every August.

Ventspils (population 52,000) is a busy port and manufacturing hub on the Baltic seacoast. From the 12th to 15th centuries, the city prospered as a ship-building center and later took advantage of a rail connection to Russia to develop export industries. In modern times, factories and a large oil refinery in Ventspils have caused severe industrial pollution.

• Latvia's Ethnic Heritage •

Most historians agree that the Latvian people originated about 4,000 years ago, when hunters, fishers, farmers, and warriors lived in the region. Latvians and Lithuanians are considered **Balts,** named for their home on the southeastern Baltic Sea. Of the numerous ancient Baltic languages, Latvian and Lithuanian are the only ones still in use.

Another ethnic group, the **Livs,** had their own independent kingdom on the Gulf of Riga until the 13th century. The first outsiders to encounter the Livs were merchants who sailed from Germany to

Markets in Latvia still offer goods from other parts of the former Soviet Union. Here, a vendor artfully cuts up a melon that was grown in the southern republic of Azerbaijan.

A woman lights votive candles at a Russian Orthodox church in the capital.

Religious freedom is guaranteed in Latvia, where communities of Protestant, Russian Orthodox, and Jewish believers live in harmony. This synagogue serves a small Jewish group in Riga.

the shores of the Gulf of Riga. These Germans called the area of Estonia and northern Latvia **Livonia** (Land of the Livs). Although a small community of Livs inhabited the Kurzeme region during Latvia's first period of independence (1918–1940), very few members of this ancient group remain today.

Of the 2.7 million people in Latvia, 52 percent are ethnic Latvians—compared to 77 percent before World War II (1939–1945). Thirty-four percent are **ethnic Russians**, many of whom were brought in by the Soviet government after Latvia's independence ended in 1940. Five percent of the population is Belarussian, and 3 percent is Ukrainian.

• Religion and Festivals •

Most Latvians follow **Lutheranism**, a Christian faith that the Germans introduced to the Baltic region in the 1500s. Roman Catholics make up one-third of the population. Catholicism flourished under the Catholic Poles, who ruled southeastern Latvia between the 16th and 18th centuries. Other denominations in Latvia include the Baptist Church and the Russian Orthodox Church.

Although many of the Jews living in Latvia at the outbreak of World War II were killed during the conflict, a small Jewish community has survived. In 1990, when religious freedoms increased, the first Jewish high school in what was then the Soviet Union opened in Riga. Latvians also founded Lutheran and Catholic schools despite the fact that Soviet authorities discouraged religious instruction.

Some festivals celebrated in Latvia have their roots in the pre-Christian era. During Ziemas Svetki, which means "winter holiday" in Latvian, participants

Latvian folk dancers performed at a festival held in Riga in 1991, the first year in which people from other countries were freely allowed to participate.

This Latvian woman wears one version of the national costume, which consists of a brightly woven skirt over a white blouse.

sing songs about the sun returning to warm the land. Latvians chant all night to scare away evil spirits during Jani, a summer festival that became St. John's Night after the population accepted Christianity. During this celebration, men wear crowns of oak branches, and women put on wreaths of wildflowers.

• Music •

Songs heard during Latvian festivals are also from a long-ago time. More than two million **dainas** —Latvian folk songs—survive. Most are four-line poems sung to ancient tunes. Folk dancing is also popular among Latvians. Many participants sing while they dance to a traditional band. Latvian folk instruments include the stringed *kokle*, the reed *stabule*, and the percussion *trejdeksnis*.

Every five years, thousands of singers come to Riga for the Latvian Song Festival. The 1990 festival featured a chorus of 28,000 singers and a five-hour parade of all the participants. For the first time since the Soviet occupation, people from other countries were able to participate in the festival.

• Health, Language, and Education •

After annexing the country, Soviet authorities built many factories in Latvia and used the republic

In a rural area of Latvia, a grandmother introduces her young grandchildren to a newborn lamb.

as a Soviet production center. The heavy industrialization gave Latvia one of the highest standards of living in the Soviet Union. The average life expectancy for Latvians is 70 years, which ranks high among the Baltic States and other eastern European countries.

Yet, Latvia has suffered many of the same problems as other former Soviet republics. The best medical attention went to important members of the Communist party, while other residents had to wait in long lines at clinics. Despite their knowledge and skill, Latvian doctors lacked important equipment. With independence, these problems now have a chance to be addressed directly.

Latvian and Russian are the two principal languages of Latvia. Russian became the country's

A sign in Latvian encourages pupils to study hard during the school year. Along with Lithuanian, Latvian is the only surviving Baltic language.

official language after the annexation. But Latvian survived among the non-Russian population and emerged once again as the country's official language in 1989. Most commercial and governmental affairs are now conducted in Latvian, and there are many Latvian newspapers and radio programs.

Education is compulsory between the ages of 6 and 17. Latvian students learn both the Latvian and Russian languages, although Russian may be dropped in the future. The largest institution of higher learning is the Latvian State University in Riga. Ten other universities exist in the republic.

Eleven-year-olds participate in a course on Latvian literature.

CHAPTER TWO

Latvia's Story

Independence has been rare in Latvian history. For centuries, foreign powers–including Russia, Germany, and Sweden–occupied the country. At one time, Latvia belonged to an alliance that also included Poland and Lithuania. Throughout history, non-Latvians have held positions of power in the region, while many Latvians became poorly paid laborers or **serfs** (workers bound to farming estates).

• *Medieval Latvia* •

In the early 12th century, Latvia consisted of four kingdoms–Kurzeme, Zemgale, Latgale, and Talava–along with a smaller territory known as Selija. The region's farms and workshops were productive, and Latvian merchants traded their goods with Arabs, Scandinavians, Romans, and Greeks. One of the most valuable resources in Latvia was **amber**, a hardened resin that could be found on the shores

In January 1991, thousands of Latvians demonstrated near the Daugava River in Riga for independence from Soviet rule.

of the Baltic. The people of the time considered this rare substance more valuable than gold. In many folk songs of the day, Latvia was called Amberland.

The resources and busy trade of the Baltic region also attracted foreign invaders, including Danish and Swedish Vikings. Christianity arrived in 1186, when the German monk Meinhard entered the country to convert the Latvians from a tradi-

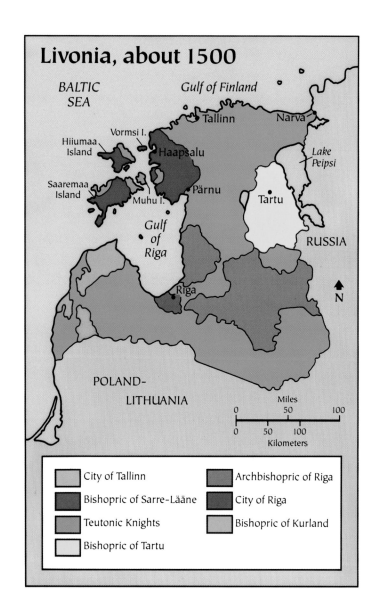

Livonia, about 1500

Legend:
- City of Tallinn
- Bishopric of Sarre-Lääne
- Teutonic Knights
- Bishopric of Tartu
- Archbishopric of Riga
- City of Riga
- Bishopric of Kurland

In the 1500s, Roman Catholic leaders and the Order of Teutonic Knights controlled Livonia—an ancient realm that stretched across Estonia and northern Latvia.

Inscriptions cover Gutman's Cave, a large sandstone formation in Sigulda—an east central Latvian town that changed hands many times during the country's history. Legends say in the 1500s a holy man named Gutman healed sick people with water from a spring inside the cave.

tional nature-based religion to the Roman Catholic faith. During the 13th century, German religious crusaders from the **Order of Teutonic Knights** overwhelmed the Latvians with superior weapons and armor. The Germans later combined northern Latvia and Estonia into Livonia.

Much of the local population had already accepted Christianity, but this mattered little to the knights, who seized town after town in the name of the Roman Catholic Church. In 1201, a Catholic bishop founded Riga as a fortified center for the German knights, who ruled Livonia for the next three centuries. In the 1500s, the **Protestant Reformation**—a religious reform movement started in Germany by Martin Luther—spread to the knights and then to many Latvians. Lutheranism became the principal faith of Livonia's people.

• The Russians Arrive •

Livonia also became a target for Russian leaders who sought an outlet on the Baltic Sea for their growing empire to the east. In 1558, the Russian czar Ivan the Terrible declared war on the German forces in the Baltic region and sent his armies to capture Livonia's ice-free ports. Fierce fighting destroyed large sections of the country, and by 1561 the kingdom of Livonia was crushed. Poland, Sweden, and Denmark then laid claim to Livonian territory and forced the czar to withdraw his troops.

By the 17th century, Poland was in control of most of Livonia. Riga fell into Swedish hands in 1629. But the powerful countries that surrounded the Baltic Sea continued to fight over the region, turning Latvia's forests and farms into battlefields.

The Great Northern War of the early 18th century was a dark period of Latvian history. This three-way conflict over the Baltic region involved the Russian czar Peter the Great, the Polish emperor Augustus, and the Swedish king Charles XII. After defeating Swedish forces at the Battle of Poltava in 1709, Peter the Great gained control of Riga and the rest of Livonia. The conflict had destroyed many farms, and thousands of Latvians lost their lives through famine and disease.

By the beginning of the 19th century, the Russian government was firmly in control of Latvia. Nevertheless, the czar allowed German landowners to hold most of the property and economic power in the country. The Latvians maintained a separate cultural identity, and the serfs who worked on the farming estates staged occasional revolts against both German landowners and the Russian czar.

Historians consider the unsuccessful 1905 revolution to be the beginning of the Latvian independence movement. Throughout the Russian Empire, people with many different political philosophies

The strategic port of Riga—located on the Baltic and crossed by the Daugava River—has access westward to the Atlantic Ocean and eastward to Russia. As a result, Russian leaders coveted the city. By the early 1700s, Riga was in Russian hands.

fought against the rule of Czar Nicholas II. Although the czar's soldiers were successful in putting down the uprising, the fires of revolt had been lit.

In the spring of 1917, another revolt in Russia toppled the czar from his throne. Later in the year, political activists known as Communists gained support among the empire's workers and soldiers. In the fall of 1917, the Communist government of Vladimir Lenin took power. Lenin sought to bring the empire's many nationalities—including the Latvians—under the control of his government. Although some Latvians were Communists, many others wanted nothing more to do with Russia.

Latvia declared its independence on November 18, 1918, while a civil war was raging between the Communist Red Army and troops loyal to the czar. Within two years, non-Communist troops had ousted the Red Army from Latvia. After much bloodshed, the Communist government agreed on August 11, 1920 to "voluntarily and forever" remove itself from Latvia. In 1922, when Lenin announced the formation of the USSR, the flag of independent Latvia was flying over the parliament building in Riga.

• A Free and Troubled Country •

In 1922, Latvian leaders adopted a new constitution that guaranteed freedom of speech and a democratically elected parliament. The document also gave equal rights to ethnic minorities, such as Germans, Russians, Poles, and Jews. The government divided the large estates once owned by Germans to create private farmland for Latvian **peasants.**

From 1920 to 1940, when Latvia was independent, the nation issued stamps and coins that commemorated Latvian leaders and historical events.

This stamp shows the Latvian coat of arms, which first came into use in the 1920s. A red lion and a silver griffin hold a shield that carries a half-sun and animal figures. The lion represents the two Latvian provinces that lie south of the Daugava River. The griffin stands for the two provinces north of the river. A ribbon in the national colors of red and white ties together the emblem.

Karlis Ulmanis, the country's first prime minister, had attended a university in the United States and had brought new political and economic ideas home to Latvia. For example, he introduced U.S. dairy-farming techniques that made Latvia an important exporter of butter. By the 1930s, however, economic decline and political instability were weakening Latvia's government, which changed hands 18 times between 1922 and 1934.

The people, who were not used to independence or to democracy, were baffled by all the turmoil. Finally, in 1934, Ulmanis dissolved parliament and banned all political parties. His opponents said this was the act of a dictator, but Ulmanis claimed these steps were necessary to keep Latvia from falling apart. In 1936, Ulmanis was also elected Latvia's president.

Karlis Ulmanis served as prime minister of the Republic of Latvia from 1918 to 1921, from 1925 to 1926, and from 1931 to 1932. In the mid-1930s, he made changes in the Latvian constitution that allowed him to be elected president in 1936. Ulmanis remained in office until 1940, when the Soviet army invaded Latvia and sent him into exile. His fate while under Soviet imprisonment is not known.

Near Riga, Latvian artists sculpted this memorial to the victims of the German occupation during World War II (1939–1945). On this site, the Germans had built a concentration camp to confine prisoners of war, Latvian Jews, and civilians suspected of anti-German activities. More than 100,000 people were murdered in the camp.

• The Horror Year •

Although it was independent, Latvia remained vulnerable to invasion from Germany and from the USSR—nations that were preparing for open conflict. In Germany, the Nazi regime of Adolf Hitler was annexing neighboring countries and building up its armed forces. The USSR under Joseph Stalin was seeking to expand into the Baltic region.

In 1939, just before the beginning of World War II, Germany and the Soviet Union signed the **Molotov-Ribbentrop Pact.** The two powers agreed to share the territory of Poland, which Germany later attacked. In a secret condition of the treaty, Germany also gave Stalin a "free hand" to annex the Baltic States.

WONDER HOW LONG THE HONEYMOON WILL LAST?

A cartoon shows the German dictator Adolf Hitler (left) arm in arm with his bride Joseph Stalin, the leader of the Soviet Union. The drawing appeared in 1939, soon after the signing of the Molotov-Ribbentrop Pact.

In June 1940, Soviet tanks entered Latvia. To save lives, the Latvian government did not resist the invasion. President Ulmanis was forced from office and sent to Siberia, a desolate region of northern Russia. His whereabouts remain unknown, but evidence indicates that he died in exile.

The next year would go down in Latvia's history as *baigais gads*—meaning "the horror year." To break Latvia's independent spirit, Soviet forces transported nearly 33,000 residents to Siberia and to other remote areas in a series of **mass deportations.** On a single night, 15,000 Latvians were sent eastward in closed railway cars. In addition, the Soviets imprisoned about 5,000 Latvian Jews.

In 1944, German tanks and soldiers retreated from Latvia, leaving rubble and ruined buildings in their wake.

After the Soviets reoccupied Latvia in 1944, they built monuments throughout the country. Put up in 1970, this statue in Riga honors Latvian riflemen who fought the Germans in World War I (1914–1918).

The summer of that year also proved disastrous for the Soviet regime. Germany staged a massive invasion of the western USSR in June, breaking the Molotov-Ribbentrop Pact. When German forces reached Latvia in July, many residents were hopeful that the Nazis would permit Latvian independence.

Hitler's government, however, viewed the country as nothing more than an occupied territory. Latvian labor and materials were sent to Germany to aid the Nazi war effort. An underground resistance movement fought to rid Latvia of the occupiers. Members of this underground caught by the Nazis were killed or sent to prison camps.

• The Return of Soviet Rule •

By 1944, Soviet victories were forcing Hitler's army to retreat westward. Soviet troops were ready to retake Latvia, whose citizens were facing yet another harsh occupation. Between August 1944 and May 1945, 240,000 Latvians—or 14 percent of the population—left the country. Some took small fishing boats across the Baltic Sea to Sweden. Others went by land or by sea toward Poland or Germany. The Soviet army caught about 50 percent of the escapees and had them killed, sent back to Latvia, or shipped to Siberia.

After the Soviet government gained firm control of Latvia, the deportations continued in an attempt to **Russify** the country. Stalin sought to impose the Russian culture and to break up the Latvian independence movement. The USSR also forced Latvian farms into the government-run **collective-farm program.** The Soviets sent 70,000 Latvians to collectives in distant Soviet republics, and ethnic Russians were brought into Latvia. In the years that followed, entire towns of non-Latvians began to appear.

Latvia's movement for independence was strengthened after Mikhail Gorbachev became leader of the Soviet Union in 1985. Gorbachev's policy of **glasnost** (meaning "openness" in Russian) eased long-standing restrictions on public speech. Glasnost resulted in a wave of anti-Soviet writings and demonstrations throughout the Baltic States.

• Resistance and Freedom •

In the late 1980s, many people began speaking their minds on Latvia's social and economic problems. By 1988, people were daring to fly the Latvian flag again. The next year, more than two million Latvians, Estonians, and Lithuanians linked hands in a human chain that stretched 400 miles (644 km) from the city of Tallinn in Estonia through Riga to the Lithuanian capital of Vilnius. During this protest, the people successfully demanded free elections. On May 4, 1990, after the Communists were voted out of power, a new Latvian parliament proclaimed the country free and independent.

Although the USSR was not willing to let go of the Baltic States, resistance within Latvia to the Soviet government continued. The opposition increased after the Soviet militia stormed Latvia's Interior Ministry on January 20, 1991.

At the same time, other republics, including Russia, were demanding elections and economic reforms. Convinced that Gorbachev could not control the republics, a group of Soviet officials tried to seize power on August 19, 1991. During this attempted overthrow—called a **coup d'état**—Soviet troops entered Riga to prevent television and radio broadcasts that might rally opposition to the coup.

On August 22, after demonstrators in Moscow (the Soviet capital) refused to obey orders to leave, the coup failed. In Latvia, protesters laid flowers

In the late 1980s and early 1990s, Latvians struggled to free their country from Soviet domination. In 1991, the central Soviet government sent troops to Riga to put down local demonstrations for self-rule. In anticipation of violent confrontations, Latvians built barricades to protect this radio station from being stormed and closed down.

at Riga's Freedom Monument and tore down a nearby statue of Lenin. The next day, Russian president Boris Yeltsin issued a decree recognizing Latvia as an independent state. Within a week, more than 30 other countries did the same. The United Nations accepted Latvia as a member in September 1991.

• *Recent Events* •

Many new political factions are competing for leadership in the new Latvian parliament. Those who were loyal to the Soviet government during the occupation now have their own political party, the Latvian Labor party. Other political groups include the Latvian Republican party, which wants Latvian emigrants from around the world to return. The Popular Front is made up of leaders of the independence movement.

Latvians will probably end up with a constitution that guarantees a strong parliament and a weak executive branch. After years of being ruled by Soviet dictators, Latvians fear the prospect of any one leader having too much power.

An even more pressing problem is Latvia's economic future. Despite independence, Latvia's economy is still closely tied to that of the former Soviet Union. Latvian leaders are trying to attract new investment and to develop trade ties with the rest of Europe. **Joint ventures** with foreign companies may also bring in investment and create jobs for Latvian workers. These new industries could better economic conditions for the Latvian people.

Latvia declared itself independent of Soviet rule in May of 1990 and noted its status with new stamps and postmarks.

CHAPTER THREE

Making
a Living
in Latvia

I n August 1991, a foreign tourist in Latvia could buy almost endlessly without running out of money. A dollar bought two pounds of sausage. A local telephone call cost one-tenth of a penny. As instability in the former Soviet Union increased, the Soviet currency—the ruble—lost more of its value. Many businesses and banks around the world now view the ruble as practically worthless.

A weak currency, although good for tourists, means hard times for Latvian workers. There is a serious shortage of housing and consumer goods. Latvians worry that the country's economy will continue to weaken if the government fails to make drastic reforms. Although Latvians have been using the ruble since the 1940 occupation, there are plans to reintroduce Latvian currency—paper money in lats, and coinage known as santims.

A worker assembles radios at one of Latvia's electronics plants. A skilled labor force and many kinds of factories have helped Latvia to become an important manufacturer of communications equipment.

People and machines harvest grain at a Latvian state-run farm. The Latvian government is breaking up many of these farms and turning over the land to private owners.

• Agriculture •

One of the Latvian government's most important economic reforms has been to break up the collective farms, where farmers worked a large, state-owned property together. Since 1989, Latvian farmers have had the right to leave the collectives and to request private land on which to raise their own crops and animals. As a result, thousands of new private farms had been established by early 1992.

Dairying and cattle raising are the chief farming activities within Latvia. The nation's fertile soil supports potatoes, peas, and cereal grains—such as barley, oats, and rye—as well as rich pasturage for livestock. Sugar beets, the raw material for refined sugar, are an important crop that may provide export income in the future.

The Latvian government has invited people who were landowners before the Soviet occupation to

Latvia's traditional cattle-raising industry supports thriving meat markets.

A woman plants seeds by hand on a plot near her home. These small fields supply much of the produce sold in Latvia's farmers' markets.

claim farms seized by the Soviets. The country's leaders hope to see 75 percent of Latvian farmland in the hands of private owners within 15 years. At one of the few successful collective farms—Adazi, about 30 miles (48 km) from Riga—a U.S. cereal company is building a plant to produce cornflakes and other products for sale in eastern Europe.

Although this farmhouse is new, its features—including peaked windows and a gently sloping roof—are in the traditional Latvian architectural style.

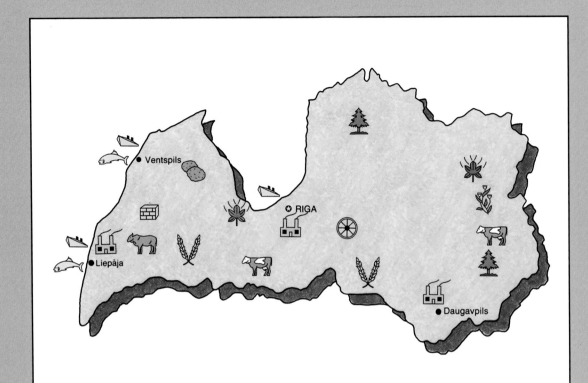

LATVIA'S ECONOMIC ACTIVITIES

Industry		Beef Cattle	
Shipbuilding		Fishing	
Building Stone		Grain and Sugar Beets	
Peat		Potatoes	
Hydroelectric Energy		Flax	
Dairy Cattle		Forestry	

• *Manufacturing* •

Latvia was heavily industrialized during the mid-20th century, when the Soviet government built plants near the country's Baltic ports. Manufacturing complexes now produce machinery, metal, timber, paper, building materials, textiles, clothing, and chemical goods. Among the chief items exported from Latvia are electric railway wagons, vans, radios, diesel engines, furniture, motorcycles, telephones, and porcelain.

To trim waste, the Latvian government plans to close some inefficient factories. In place of these formerly state-owned industries, Latvians hope to develop new private factories that will produce profitable exports.

Even before the attempted coup sped up the independence process, Latvia's leaders were encouraging private businesses to replace state-run firms. By 1992, more than 1,000 independently operated enterprises existed in the country. The number of farmers' markets and street vendors also increased to meet the demand for food and consumer goods, which no longer have to be sold through government-owned stores.

Workers stitch cloth in one of Riga's shoe factories. If freed of state control and modernized, many Latvian firms will be able to make products that meet the local demand for consumer goods and that also compete in international markets.

Giant cranes load cargo onto freighters in the commercial harbor of Riga. One of the largest ports in the Baltic region, Riga is the key to Latvia's future as an international trading center.

• Trade and Energy •

Latvia's Baltic Sea ports have been among the nation's most important economic resources. Over the centuries, invaders have targeted Riga, Ventspils, and other harbors to gain easy access to other countries on the Baltic Sea. Riga and Ventspils became important outlets for grain shipments from Ukraine (a former Soviet republic) while the Soviets occupied Latvia. If enough money is invested to aid the undertaking, a third port in Liepāja may also be used for cargo transportation. Latvia's large fishing fleet, which brings in mostly cod and herring, calls at large and small harbors along the Baltic coast.

Latvia's limited natural resources include building stone, timber, refined sand for optical lenses, and clays for bricks and tiles. **Peat**—decayed, compacted vegetation—is found near the Gulf of Riga and provides fuel for power stations in the country.

Latvia has large hydroelectric plants on the Daugava River. Geothermal electric plants, which generate power from heated underground water, exist near Liepāja and on the coast north of Riga. Nevertheless, Latvia produces no oil, natural gas, or coal. An important Soviet oil pipeline ends in Ventspils, and Latvians hope to work out an agreement in which they maintain the pipeline in return for a percentage of its profits. This arrangement could also reduce Latvia's dependence on foreign oil imports.

A hydroelectric dam on the Daugava River generates power for Latvian homes and factories. With a lack of fossil fuels, such as oil and coal, Latvia must rely on waterpower for much of its electricity.

Truckers provide black-market gasoline from their tankers to a needy car owner. Fuel shortages force many Latvian drivers to seek gas on the expensive—and illegal—black market.

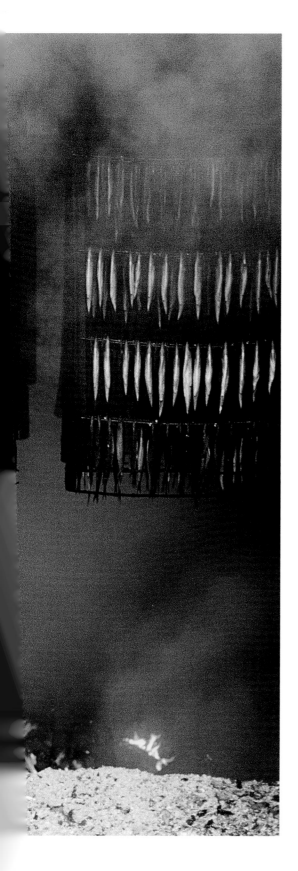

CHAPTER FOUR

What's Next for Latvia?

W ith a lack of natural resources, Latvia needs solid trading relationships with its neighbors to prosper. Having fought for independence as a team, the Baltic States remain close, and their governments may make the new currencies in the region interchangeable. Yet, there is little desire in Latvia to form a federation with its Baltic allies, since all three nations just gained independence from the Soviet Union.

Other states once dominated by the Soviet government have also been sympathetic to Latvia. In the summer of 1991, for example, the Czech and Slovak Federal Republic agreed to a trade pact, and Latvia and Poland have signed a declaration of friendship and mutual cooperation.

Latvia's leaders are also looking west for their future diplomatic and economic ties. The Scandinavian nations of Iceland and Denmark were among

At a fishery in Jurmala, a woman arranges fresh Baltic fish on racks for drying and smoking.

FAST FACTS ABOUT LATVIA

Total Population	2.7 million
Ethnic Mixture	52 percent Latvian 34 percent Russian 5 percent Belarussian 3 percent Ukrainian 2 percent Polish
CAPITAL and Major Cities	RIGA Daugavpils, Ventspils
Major Languages	Latvian, Russian
Major Religions	Lutheranism Russian Orthodoxy
Year of inclusion in USSR	1940
Status	Fully independent, sovereign state; member of United Nations since 1991

the first foreign countries to recognize the newly independent state. On August 27, 1991, five days after the coup failed, Denmark sent the first official foreign diplomat to Riga since 1940.

Since many western European nations already have trade agreements among themselves, some Latvians would rather form new commercial relationships in Asia. They point out that countries like Taiwan, South Korea, and Singapore could use Latvian lumber, fish, vegetables, and building materials.

This German-Latvian joint venture produces colorful athletic shoes.

Latvians also realize that the former republics of the Soviet Union need to cooperate to trade their goods. In 1990, treaties involving exchanges of cultural and scientific information were signed with Belarus, Moldova, Ukraine, Armenia, Kyrghyzstan, and Turkmenistan. Latvia also finalized an economic agreement with Russia in January 1991.

• *Who is a Latvian?* •

Perhaps the nation's most challenging debate involves the qualifications for Latvian citizenship. Many former Communists argue that every resident of the country should be eligible. Others believe the right should be reserved for those who were living in the country in 1940 and their descendants.

The plight of ethnic Russians in Latvia, who make up 34 percent of the population, is even more complicated. Many of the laborers in Latvia's

Economic unity among the Baltic States is a key to their financial survival. Here, Anatoliss Gorbunovs of Latvia (left), Arnold Rüütel of Estonia (middle), and Vytautas Landsbergis of Lithuania (right) sign an accord that pledges their nations to economic and military cooperation.

factories are Russians, while both Latvians and non-Latvians work as managers. Only one-fifth of the country's non-Latvian residents speak Latvian, however. Even though many Russians supported the independence movement, some Latvians condemn them as outsiders who have no respect for Latvian culture.

Many schools and businesses are now using the Latvian language instead of Russian. Yet, nearly half of the population speak Russian as their first language, and Russian will probably not disappear completely. Latvia is likely to remain a nation of two languages, as its people struggle to understand their past and to build toward their future.

Latvian students enjoy a wintry walk in an old section of Riga. Schools in Latvia have replaced Russian with Latvian as the language of their classrooms and textbooks.

Russian soldiers often patrolled the streets of Riga before Latvia gained independence from the Soviet Union. Under a recent agreement with Russia, these troops are scheduled to leave by the end of 1992.

With a Latvian father and a Russian mother, these bilingual (two-language) children symbolize a future in which ethnic Latvians and ethnic Russians live together peacefully.

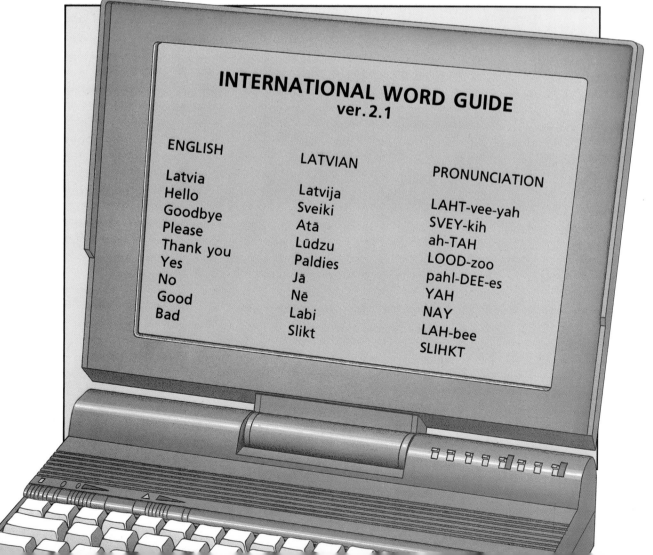

INTERNATIONAL WORD GUIDE
ver. 2.1

ENGLISH	LATVIAN	PRONUNCIATION
Latvia	Latvija	LAHT-vee-yah
Hello	Sveiki	SVEY-kih
Goodbye	Atā	ah-TAH
Please	Lūdzu	LOOD-zoo
Thank you	Paldies	pahl-DEE-es
Yes	Jā	YAH
No	Nē	NAY
Good	Labi	LAH-bee
Bad	Slikt	SLIHKT

acid rain: rainfall that contains pollutants from the air. When combined with water, these pollutants form acids.

amber: a hard, yellowish petrified resin from the sap of pine trees that can be polished and used in jewelry and other ornaments.

annex: to add a country or territory to the domain of another nation by force.

Balt: a person living in one of the nations along the Baltic Sea, including Lithuania, Latvia, and Estonia.

Baltic States: a common term for Estonia, Latvia, and Lithuania, all of which are independent republics that border the Baltic Sea in northern Europe.

collective-farm program: a system of large agricultural estates worked by a group. The workers usually received a portion of the farm's harvest as wages. On a Soviet collective farm, the central government owned the land, buildings, and machinery.

Communist: a person who supports Communism —an economic system in which the government owns all farmland and the means of producing goods in factories.

coup d'état: French words meaning "blow to the state" that refer to a swift, sudden overthrow of a government.

crusader: a Christian soldier who waged wars of conquest in the 11th, 12th, and 13th centuries.

daina: a Latvian folk song made up of a short poem that is sung to an ancient melody.

ethnic Latvian: a person whose ethnic heritage is Balto-Finnish and who speaks Latvian.

ethnic Russian: a person whose ethnic heritage is Slavic and who speaks Russian.

Modern structures shelter dairy cattle at the Adazi collective, a successful state-owned farm that has begun joint ventures with foreign companies.

An illustration from Lacplesis—*the children's tale that became a symbol of Latvia's struggle for independence—shows the hero attacking a bear.*

glasnost: meaning "openness," the Russian name for a policy of the late 1980s that eased restrictions on writing and speech.

industrialize: to build and modernize factories for the purpose of manufacturing a wide variety of consumer goods and machinery.

joint venture: an economic partnership between a locally owned business and a foreign-owned company.

Lacplesis: an old Latvian children's tale that became a popular symbol of Latvia's modern drive for independence from the Soviet Union.

Liv: a person from the kingdom of Livonia, which existed along the Baltic coast until the 13th century.

Livonia: an ancient realm that included Estonia and northern Latvia.

Lutheranism: the Christian Protestant sect that was brought to Latvia by Germans in the 16th century. Most ethnic Latvians are Lutherans.

mass deportation: a large-scale, forced movement of people from one place to another.

Molotov-Ribbentrop Pact: a political agreement negotiated by Vyacheslav Molotov of the Soviet Union and Joachim von Ribbentrop of Germany. Signed in 1939, the agreement said that the two nations would not attack one another or interfere with one another's military and political activities. A secret part of the pact stated that Germany would give the USSR a free hand to annex the Baltic region.

Order of Teutonic Knights: a German-Christian military organization that took over the Baltic region in the mid-1300s.

peasant: a small landowner or landless farm worker.

peat: decayed vegetation that has become densely packed down in swamps and bogs. Peat can be cut, dried, and burned as fuel.

Protestant Reformation: a religious movement of the 1500s that sought to reform the Roman Catholic Church.

Russian Empire: a large kingdom that covered present-day Russia as well as areas to the west and south. It existed from roughly the mid-1500s to 1917.

Russify: to make Russian by imposing the Russian language and culture on non-Russian peoples.

serf: a rural worker under the feudal landowning system, which tied people to a farming estate for life. Serfs had few rights and owed their labor and a portion of their harvest to the landowner.

Union of Soviet Socialist Republics (USSR): a large nation in eastern Europe and northern Asia that consisted of 15 member-republics. It existed from 1922 to 1991.

United Nations: an international organization formed after World War II whose primary purpose is to promote world peace through discussion and cooperation.

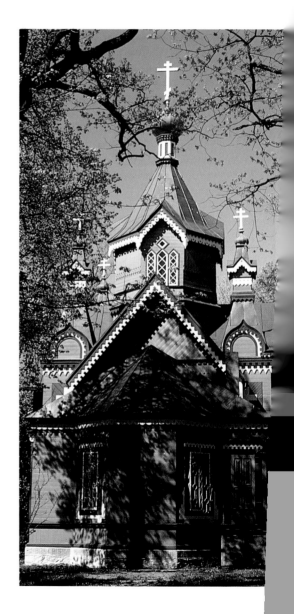

This Russian Orthodox church lies within the grounds of a health spa near Riga. Russian rulers introduced the Russian Orthodox religion to the Baltic region as part of their effort to Russify Latvia. Nevertheless, most Latvians continued to follow Lutheranism, their traditional Protestant faith.

Agriculture, 13, 27, 30–32, 35, 40–41, 52–53

Architecture, 10–11, 41

Arts, 12, 33

Atlantic Ocean, 12, 16, 30–31

Baltic Sea, 12–13, 16, 18, 20, 28, 30, 35, 44

Baltic States, 12, 17, 20–21,24, 28, 30, 33, 36, 44, 47, 49, 54. See also Estonia; Lithuania

Belarus, 12–13, 20, 49

Cities, 17, 20, 29, 47. See also Riga

Citizenship, claims to, 49

Climate, 16

Communists, 7–8, 24, 31, 36, 49

Constitution, 31, 37

Crusaders, 17, 29

Daugava River, 13, 20, 30, 32, 44–45

Daugavpils, 20

Demonstrations, 26–27, 36

Denmark, 30, 47–48

Economy, 8, 32, 36–37, 38–45, 49

Education, 17, 22, 25, 50

Elections, 32, 36

Energy, 44–45

Environmental concerns, 12, 18–19, 20

Estonia, 12, 21, 28–29, 36, 49. See also Baltic States

Ethnic groups, 8, 17, 20–21, 31, 49, 51

Europe, 7–8, 20, 24, 35, 37, 41. See also Denmark; Germany; Sweden

Exports, 20, 32, 40, 43

Festivals, 20, 22–23

Finland, 12

Fishing, 44, 46–47

Forests, 13, 15, 18

Freedom Monument, 6–7, 8, 37

Germany, 20–21, 27, 29, 30, 33–35

Gorbachev, Mikhail, 36

Gorbunovs, Anatoliss, 49

Health, 23–24, 30

History, 27–37
  annexation, 9, 23, 25, 33
  independence, 8–9, 12, 21, 24, 26–27, 30–33, 35–37, 50, 53
  Livonia, 8, 21, 28–30
  recent events, 37, 47–51
  Russian rule, 16, 26–27, 30–31, 35–37

Imports, 45

Independence, 8–9, 12, 21, 24, 26–27, 30–33, 35–37, 50, 53

Industry. See Manufacturing

Ivan IV (the Terrible), 30

Jews, 21–22, 31, 33–34

Lacplesis, 11–12, 53

Languages, 17, 20, 24–25, 50–51

Latvia
  boundaries, size, and location of, 12–13
  government of, 9, 31–32, 37, 40–41, 43
  population of, 21

Lenin, Vladimir, 31, 37

Life expectancy, 24

Lithuania, 12, 20, 27, 36, 49. See also Baltic States

Livonia, 8, 21, 28–30

Manufacturing, 7, 17–20, 23–24, 37, 38–39, 40, 43

Maps and charts, 14–15, 28, 42, 48, 51

Molotov-Ribbentrop Pact, 33, 35

Money, 39, 47

Moscow, 36

Music, 11, 20, 23, 28

Natural resources, 27–28, 45

Young Latvians pass the afternoon playing with Barbie dolls.

People
   education, 17, 22, 25, 50
   ethnic groups, 8, 17, 20–21, 31, 49, 51
   health, 23–24, 30
   languages, 17, 20, 24–25, 50–51
   religion, 21–22, 28–29, 54
Peter I (the Great), 30
Poland, 20, 27, 30, 33, 35, 47
Pollution. *See* Environmental concerns
Population, 21
Ports, 16, 20, 30, 43–44. *See also* Riga
Religion, 21–22, 28–29, 54
Republics, former Soviet, 12–13, 20, 24, 44, 49. *See also* Belarus; Russia
Riga, 5–8, 10–11, 16, 17, 21–23, 25, 26–27, 29–31, 35–36, 40, 43–45, 48, 50, 54

Riga, Gulf of, 12, 16, 20–21, 45
Rivers and lakes, 13, 18. *See also* Daugava River
Russia, 12–13, 20, 27, 30–31, 34, 36, 49, 50
Russian Empire, 7–9, 30–31
Shipping, 20, 44
Siberia, 34–35
Soviet Union, 7–9, 11, 22, 23–24, 33–37, 39, 41, 43, 47, 50
Stalin, Joseph, 33, 35
Standard of living, 24
Sweden, 12, 27, 30, 35
Teutonic Knights, Order of, 28–29
Topography, 12–15
Trade, 17, 20, 27–28, 37, 44, 47–49
Transportation, 20, 44
Ulmanis, Karlis, 32, 34
Union of Soviet Socialist Republics (USSR). *See* Soviet Union
United Nations, 9, 37

United States, 32, 41
Ventspils, 18–19, 20, 44–45
Warfare, 30–31
Yeltsin, Boris, 37

• *Photo Acknowledgments* •

Photographs are used courtesy of: pp. 1, 8 (left), 12 (right), 16 (left and right), 17, 20, 21 (left and right), 23, 24, 25 (left and right), 33 (left), 40 (bottom), 41 (top and bottom), 43, 44, 45 (left and right), 49 (top), 55, Jeff Greenberg; pp. 2, 30, 50 (left), © Michael Reagan / FPG International; pp. 5, 6, 8 (right), 9, 10, 12 (left), 15, 29, 31 (top and bottom), 32 (left), 36, 37, 50 (right), 54, John Polis; p. 13, © Anna Cloped / REA / SABA; p. 18, © Shepard Sherbell / SABA; pp. 22, 35, 38, 51 (top), 52, TASS / SOVFOTO; p. 26, © Ilkka Ranta / Lehtikuva Oy / SABA; p. 32 (right), University of Nebraska, Love Library Special Collections; p. 33 (right), Independent Picture Service; p. 34, © FPG International; pp. 40 (top), 49 (bottom), NOVOSTI / SOVFOTO; p. 46, © Bill Foley / Stock South; p. 53, Girts Vilks. Maps and charts: pp. 14–15, 42, J. Michael Roy; pp. 28, 48, 51, Laura Westlund.

Covers: (Front) © Fred Salaff / FPG International; (Back): Jeff Greenberg